Moments in Time

Moments In Time
Reflections

RONNIE JORDAN

iUniverse, Inc.
Bloomington

MOMENTS IN TIME
REFLECTIONS

Copyright © 2011 by Ronnie Jordan.

All rights reserved. No part of this book may be used or reproduced by any means, graphic, electronic, or mechanical, including photocopying, recording, taping or by any information storage retrieval system without the written permission of the publisher except in the case of brief quotations embodied in critical articles and reviews.

iUniverse books may be ordered through booksellers or by contacting:

iUniverse
1663 Liberty Drive
Bloomington, IN 47403
www.iuniverse.com
1-800-Authors (1-800-288-4677)

Because of the dynamic nature of the Internet, any web addresses or links contained in this book may have changed since publication and may no longer be valid. The views expressed in this work are solely those of the author and do not necessarily reflect the views of the publisher, and the publisher hereby disclaims any responsibility for them.

Any people depicted in stock imagery provided by Thinkstock are models, and such images are being used for illustrative purposes only.
Certain stock imagery © Thinkstock.

ISBN: 978-1-4620-5310-0 (sc)
ISBN: 978-1-4620-5311-7 (ebk)

Printed in the United States of America

iUniverse rev. date: 10/13/2011

Our Father

My Dear Supporters, I sincerely believe God is in me and in you. This is one of my reasons why, there was this moment in my life where right before he passed, I witnessed my grandfather praying and singing in his sleep. This was a powerful moment in his life and mine. I can recall as a child listening to him singing hymns and listening to him praying every night. I too pray each night and thank God for all he has done for me and will do for me. I ask that you take a moment and pray with me so he will bless you as well; Dear heavenly Father I want to thank you for all you have done for me in my life and continue to do for me. Father God you have always loved me regardless of my faults and have never looked down on me. I realize that I have fallen short of your glory but I pray that you continue to uplift me and to use me to help someone. Father God I thank you for blessing my family and all those that have come into my life, and I thank you for your grace and your mercy because you choose to show me and those I love favor. Father God continue to help me grow where I fall short, where I am weak and whenever I want to give up. Bless all who read and hear these words for it is our belief in Jesus that we have all come this far. Father God help me to continue to be an inspiration to someone even though I have my own faults and am a work in progress as well. Let your light shine in me and shine through me so that all will know that you can and will do what you say as long as we believe in you and put you first. For it is in Jesus' name I pray.

Amen

My Thanks To All

When I think about the first book of poetry I wrote and realize how well it has been received, I am amazed and truly blessed. I sincerely want to thank all my family and friends who have encouraged and supported me. I never imagined my poetry would touch so many people as well as inspire them to pursue their own goals and it is very humbling to see. This book is one which I feel will encourage all my readers to look even further inside themselves as they realize anything is possible if you try and believe in your pursuit with all your heart. I want to give special thanks to my children, Demarcus, Stensen, and Danielle. I especially want to thank my wife Sherrel for staying on me. A special thanks to Francis, my sister, my aunts, my cousins, and my nieces for inspiring me to do what I love. To you Josephine Jordan and John Henry Copeland, thanks so much mom and granddad for all you did for me and for being my role models. I now carry you inside my heart forever because I could never repay you for what you've done and continue to do for me even though you're gone. I love you both and miss you dearly.

Dear readers, I would love to hear from you so if you wish, I can be reached at ronniejordan62@yahoo.com

THERE AIN'T NO WORDS

There ain't no words that I can say to describe how I felt

when you left me forever that day.

There ain't no words to describe how I feel when sometimes

I gaze up into the sky, I know you are in heaven so I don't ask

God the reason why.

There ain't no words to describe how helpless I felt as I saw you

lying there, as my heart kept screaming I love you and said I will

always care.

There ain't no words to describe how I felt the last time we would

talk, all I need to know was you were my momma and no one was at

fault.

There ain't no words to describe how much you sacrificed, for both me

and my sister, it never bothered you to give us so much of your life.

There ain't no words to describe how often I dream, dream of the

woman I loved to call momma for so many years, a woman

named Josephine.

There ain't no words to describe the many gifts that you possessed, all were gifts from God for you deserved nothing less.

There ain't no words to describe how I hurt when I talk to you from beside your grave, I guess what does come to mind is someone very special that God had made.

I am sure I will spend many waking moments writing things about you, many things I already know, others I will have heard, but to truly say what you mean to me momma . . . . There ain't no words.

MORNING

$\mathcal{E}$ach day the promise of life is brought to fore by a new morning. New adventures, creations, ideas and journeys are brought to life by the warm bath of the morning's glowing sun, O' what a wonderful morning.

The song called unity, the song of the people, is sung in harmony when life stirs the soul of a nation in the morning. This song embraces all that is alive in us and touches the heart of every soul in the world.

The poor and the prosperous seem one and the same when morning comes, both feeling the joy of an awakened nation that is embracing a prosperous and bright future. It is here all can bear witness to the many gifts morning has bestowed upon us as a great nation, for color is not important in the morning, just rejoicefulness for being among the many singing the song of unity.

Our nation has always traveled the river of determination, though It may slow, it awakens with renewed vitality when the morning stirs its dormant soul. This river gives life to a nation of colors, beautiful rainbows and waterfalls casting breathtaking hues throughout a determined society whose hearts and souls sing unity.

Let us all join hands and go to the river of unity and gather under the future tree. Let us enjoy its fruit of togetherness. Let us sit upon its many branches of wisdom and let us embrace its proud and powerful trunk for it is the foundation of this great tree that holds together that which makes our beautiful nation a beacon to the world. And when the night falls upon us, let us all look to the heavens and ask God for yet another beautiful and inspiring morning.

OLD MAN

He sat in his porch chair, listening to the old wood floor
sing its familiar song, he'd just rock to and fro, age no longer
his adversary, just the way everyone's life has to go.
Riches he never had but for all he had done in his life, things
hadn't been so bad, and he felt he had done well. Some of
his children, family and many of his friends had long gone on,
but even at 91 years of age life for him was still going strong.
A friendly wave to him was always met with a wave back, a
reminder that he was still important to someone and he liked
that.

The one thing he so dearly wished for, longed for, was the wife
who had gone long before, a yearning that always brought a tear to
his eyes for his love for her was still strong, this woman he did adore.
The brightness of the sky matched the hues of his eyes, still
sparkling after such a long journey.
The one lesson he always left when talking to his fellow man was always
do right by everybody, always do what you can, yea do what you can.
As always he laid his head aside to rest though this time his eyes
whispered to him sleep forever . . . . old man.

DREAMS

If a person has the time to wish,
then he has the time to dream.
If a person has the time to hope,
then he has the time to fulfill his
dream.

Dreams are the beginning of a desired
journey that many have in their hearts
and hope to someday accomplish.
Oh yes, the pitfalls that await us on the
road to our dream are numerous and
we often want to yield, never yield, for
an undaunted spirit shall always succeed.

As we strive for success, boldness and
determination are there for all who pursue their dream.
Courage and perseverance is
there for all who hold on to their dream,
and knowledge and wisdom is there for all
who dare to achieve . . . . their dream.

MISSISSIPPI DELTA

This OL' delta, now a desolate and weary land, provides little work for the downtroddened man. A place where cotton is still the kingsman, its softness still picked by wretched hands.

It has windswept fields, most of its shelter gone, what little there is left for the poor people, are broken spirits, yearning souls living in decrepit and dilapidated homes.

These poor people bare a scattered tongue that echoes words from a past long ago heard. A dialect borne of the deep south, listing words that resonate behind crooked teeth inside a ragged mouth.

Little children, babies with hungry bellies searching mothers for something to eat. Nourishment coming by way of a mother searching for anything to feed them as hunger disturbs their sleep.
Little knowledge is learned for tomorrow abandoned the delta long ago. Those minds that are broadened never return so there is nothing to share, these souls of the delta have seen it so many times where a new day of hope seems to always turn into a day of despair.

As it will, the howling winds of change force grimness back towards its darkened shame, back inside its ugly lair, so just hold on, triumph is coming, people of the Mississippi delta for those of us that see, truly does care.

LORD TALK TO ME

Dear Lord the bridge to heaven appears broken,
I cannot come home to the promised land. The Lord
said child never will there be anything I cannot mend,
believe in thine heart and come home my child.

Lord the spirits of wickedness are saying they will never
allow me to cross, I know not whether to go forth or
hide in fear. The Lord said, fear not my child for I made
all of creation, thy spirits of wickedness will never
conquer thee.

Lord I am trying but my feet are tattered, worn and weary
from life's many travels. I cannot take another step Lord.
The Lord said my child your tired soul rests upon the shoulders
of the Holy Spirit, ask and it will carry you.

Lord, I finally can look towards heaven with clasped hands
for the bridge is paved with silver and gold. My feet are healed
anew and the Holy Spirit is holding me. Lord the spirits of
wickedness have turned and fled. We are crossing the bridge
and are coming to the promised land.

MY NEW HOME

Look up, look up dear family and friends, see my
new home?
Tis a place of angels, silver streams and gold, O'
heaven is so beautiful.
Dry your teary eyes and listen to the sounds of the
glorious trumpets caressing one's soul.
Reach up high and feel the gentle breeze that is
now my spirit.
Smile for me for I am happy and forever free.
Place, place your hand over your hearts. You see,
my spirit lies within you and never will I part.
When you lie down to rest, let your memories roam,
as always I am thinking of you here in heaven, someday
your new home.
Always know and always see, that no matter where you
are, I am with you and will always be.

REMEMBRANCE

O' how we laughed and how we cried, cried and we laughed, beautiful memories of things from our past.
Those wonderful memories of our times together under the willow tree, talking hour upon hour while letting our thoughts run free.
Just thinking about the silly things we did sometimes made us weep, sometimes made us laugh, beautiful memories now when we think about the past.
Many times we would ask does forever really end, God always answered no for it is where heaven begins.
As life moves us on those moments we will never forget for we carry them in our hearts now. Special times of . . . . remembrance.

WHAT IF JESUS

What if Jesus had asked God to spare him
for our sins?
The world would be even more terrible,
only enemies and no friends.
What if Jesus took away all our daily blessings?
our lives would be mere shadows, dark window
dressings.
What if Jesus never cured any sickness or disease?
Death would be our only companion, running
rampant through our lives with ease.
What if Jesus allowed our hearts to be forever cold?
Hell would be our home for only heaven takes Christian
souls.
What if Jesus said death to all sinners? There would be
no one who could repent because we all have not
always been Christian winners.
We need not ask what if of Jesus, his word is guaranteed,
the Bible tells us so, you see it is the reason we succeed.

IF YOU CAN

If blame is placed all around you and upon you for ten thousand days and you remain steadfast as your blamer becomes more adamant about your supposed errors and transgressions. Yet you realize that justice has wings that will carry you forth when conflict is allowed to accompany them and their angry deeds against you. If your patience is constantly put to test and yet you embrace such a test while realizing many would enjoy your rise to anger as they eagerly pursue you and attempt to attack your calmness.

If wisdom urges you to become great though you do not bask in your greatness and if you can conquer all your obstacles and appreciate all your accomplishments while remaining humble with either. If you can walk with your enemy and not smite him for speaking untruths and slanders against you knowing he has wrong you, yet you still quench his thirst.

If you can maintain your wits whenever the tempest swirls around you, as those near you quiver in fear, yet smiles of bravado is not your countenance because steadfastness considers you fine company while allowing humbleness to consider you a gentleman.

If you can relinquish all your trinkets, all your treasures to those with even more and if it bothers you nary as you realize starting anew is but a simple task as you trudge forward. If all push you backwards in the race for success and you cut no corners while forcing your spirit and your soul to try harder as victory screams at you though you grasp hold to nothing, and your eyes open to a failed triumph, you still whisper I've done it.

If you can rise above the venomous vitriol while all those around you are desperately seeking your shortcomings, yet when none are found they are then created by those with envy, or if you can walk side by side with leaders of great nations and still embrace the vagabond as you brush aside criticisms from any and all. If forgiveness is never held by your lips while you release to the masses with unrequited vigor that forgiveness. If you can, then you will have risen above all that life has placed before you and are greatest among them all.

FORGIVE ME

The storm inside her heart is gathering with a fierceness
never before seen. Eternal promises given you by her, yet your
eyes and faithfulness are slowly being stolen by another.
Are her fruits any more delectable than mine she asks?
Never you dare say tis the appeal and the mystery you think. Mystery
is what stirs the soul to seek. Aye such a treasure where
many a man believes to himself no other has yet discovered?
Though dare you wish to discern, the treasure you seek is already
secured by an unwary foe, his security too, is threatened, her wry smile
a telling clue. Tomorrow brings a new beginning for forgiveness, yet
lessons learned go unnoticed and heartfelt apologies go unheard.
The untruths told to your beloved by you are the only discussions she
hears and she says good-bye. Your pleas of forgive me go unnoticed
for she never heard you say—please don't go.

GRANDMOTHER

When I see your face, there is no better place than
to be in your presence, to lose you makes my heart
shudder, what a treasure you are grandmother.
When late at night as I cry out in fright, your soothing
kiss becomes the guardian of my soul, protection
from the evils lurking in my dreams. To lose you makes
my heart shudder, what a treasure you are grandmother.
When better days it seems, are only in my dreams, you
would say pray and press on my child, you will receive
your blessing. To lose you makes my heart shudder, what
a treasure you are grandmother. When at last I fall asleep
and I hear you weep, I lay my head upon your breast,
fear not for I will always give my very best. Grandmother I
realize that I have sometimes been so much trouble,
yet you loved me so, what a loving treasure you are,
grandmother.

MOMMA DON'T CRY

Christmas is here again and all I got is me and my best
friend. Santa won't be here again and I don't know
why.
My momma sits there in the corner and starts to
cry.
Sometimes she screams and says she wants to die.
I don't want her life to end, I don't have no one else
and there is always tomorrow and we can try again.
Look here momma, don't you cry, when I grow up
I'll give you the sky.
Show me again your pretty smile, things will be
alright in just a little while.
Look momma, all we need to do is give it another try,
'cause no way am I gonna stand here and watch you
cry.

ILLEGAL TENDER

Life's innocent, tender beings sometimes do not remain this way when the moon becomes full. The moon eager to view unsavory men happy to triumph their unspoiled temples. Lustful characters aching to invade young ladies whose precious treasures are soon to be ravaged. Too young to understand there is a better way of life, these innocent angels are allowing others to profit from their unspoiled gift. These unwise minds easily controlled by thinking this financial gain will always come with little effort. Underage women of the night they have become. With no one to guide them, the streetlight is fast becoming their beacon. Soon time will reveal this life will never allow success, will seldom allow hope, for a street angel has few meaningful mentors. These destitute young souls soon realize they have now become their own financial institution, their bodies purveyors of finance, their lives turned into illegal tender.

MY MOTHER

You're the most beautiful first person I saw upon my arrival in this world, your joyous tears giving me my first wash. Though it would take nine months to see you, it seems as though we have been together forever. Time passes on and the years turned me into a grownup, someone mother who is not ashamed to say I would truly enjoy a hug from you. Though graying in your years, you are still as lovely as the nightingale, as graceful as the swan and as gentle as a peaceful summer night. The word friend is often stated in error, for in reality it really means mother. There is no better friend than you. You have always did the right things, you always say the right things, because you are the best thing that ever happened to me.
I will always call heaven in hope of hearing your voice . . . my dear mother.

BLACK BUTTERFLY

Black butterfly, hear my cry. How graceful you glide
up there in the clear blue sky. Yes, O' black butterfly,
I hear your angelic and beautiful wings. They whistle
an enchanting and melodic song, O' how I love to
hear them sing. Soft and gentle is your majestic flight,
where from flower to flower you land and so very
light. When being chased, you flee with glee for your
soul is so pure it can only be free. Now beautiful and
graceful black butterfly, soar away, soar away into
the clear blue sky.

A WOMAN'S WORK

When his soul is broken she is always standing right there, for if she wasn't his spirit would be too hard to repair.

When her family is crying because life has given them a a terrible path, she will gather them around her, kneel and pray, for she knows it will not last.

When no food is to be found and hunger becomes a friend, she still finds something to prepare a warm meal, while never letting anyone see how much she cries inside nor how ashamed her heart feels.

When her children are sick and no money is to be found, no doctor can be called upon nor seen, she always calls on the name of Jesus and marvels at the wonderful healing he always brings.

When the going gets really tough and she wants to give up and scream, she fights on for she knows God will provide an answer, maybe in a vision or maybe in a dream.
She knows life will sometimes be hard, she knows things in life sometimes hurt, but she also knows with God on her side, she is able to do . . . . a woman's work.

SO MANY TEARS

High expectations of our children is the reason many endure as a parent. Love it seems sometimes replaced by a yearning to achieve personal dreams through them. This love for the child diminished because of their falling short of our goals. Those hoped for memories now languish in the past yet again, replaced by cutting words because the results hoped for are not achieved. Parental criticism bringing with it so many tears within the heart of the child. Dreams of making a parent proud are dashed to the wayside when too much of a burden is placed on a young soul, their perceived failure brings so many tears. It is more than understood that the parent is the foundation that guides the child on to success. Sometimes in life the parent will lack those gifts which are necessary to help their child to achieve. Though it is here where the small shoulders of the child are forced to carry forth the dreams of the parent. If they fail to live up to expectations, their effort often ends in pain and O' so many tears.

THIEF OF HEARTS

To have given you my life would be far better than your destroying my trusting heart. You see death would have been more kind to me.

Like a thief in the night you came into my life with a false promise of love and till death we will part.

I reached out to you in earnest for I thought I knew you would be there to comfort and care for me when life chose not to show me favor.

No, never would you be so kind for like a thief in the night, you only came to steal from me, to rob from me, to pilfer from me the one possession that I have, you took with you my heart and seasoned it with betrayal.

No a true crime was not committed, for you were most welcome. Though I should have known, I allowed myself to be subdued by your false promises, and allowed you to crush our dream of forever by stealing away the trust in my heart.

MOTHER

If this world were ours, we would give you
all the secrets of the deep blue sea, give you
all it's hidden treasures whatever they might
be. For never will there be another, tis why
we love you dear sweet mother.

So often we would be sad, just wanting to cry,
but upon your chest our heads would lie. So
lovingly you would say, you are better than
the rest and in my eyes you will forever be the
best. Never will there be another, tis why we
love you dear sweet mother.

And when the day comes to an end and we know
not what to do, your endearing and encouraging
words would always help us through. From where
we will go, to where we have been, you have been
with us O' wonderful friend. Never will there be
another, no not like you . . . . dear sweet mother.

SHOESHINE MAN

One dollar sir will get your shoes a great shine.
You do fine work fella, fine work indeed. Here
take two dollars instead.

Many years go by and still he's shining shoes.
Daddy why do you still shine shoes? It's all I
know son but it provides for us.

Many more years go by and he's still shining shoes.
A young man asks, daddy why do you still shine
shoes? It's all I know son but it provides for us.

Listen you never went hungry, you always had a
decent home and I paid for your learning. I hear
you are a doctor now.

Son see it's not what you do, but enjoying what
you do, shining shoes is what I know how to do
son. It's not too bad for an old black man, no
not too bad for an old shoeshine man.

MY FATHER

A pointed pleasure secretes into her veins, what once she thought was joy, now causes constant pain. A stranger who cared enough to comfort her broken soul, said I am your Father.

When her world was constantly filled with strife, and those she loved could care less if she took her life, a stranger who cared enough to comfort her broken soul, said I am your Father.

When what she thought was the love of her life was only an ugly lie, and she then opened her wrists and wanted to die, a stranger who cared enough to comfort her broken soul, said I am your Father.

When life forced her to live out on the streets, and her body was the only treasure she could use to eat, a stranger who cared enough to comfort her broken soul, said I am your Father.

Puzzled, she said good stranger, thank you for being there through all my troubles, I am told my father has long passed and you are not his double. It was then and there he started to glow and said to her there is something I want you to know. Whenever your troubles proved to be too hard and life would not show you favor, I heard your cry. For I am your Father, many call me Jesus my child, I am your . . . . Savior.

NOBODY CARED

When the worst of your fears became a reality, nobody cared.
When the world saw your broken spirit, nobody cared.
When you finally were strong enough to stare defeat in the face and announced your presence, nobody cared.
And when you stole away into the night with never a mention you were gone, never a search for your flight, you knew nobody cared.
But O' whenever you look over your shoulder and see me standing there, you will see that somebody cares, and that somebody is me.

SELF

Retrospect would often visit me for days on end. Reminding me of errors in my spirit and in my deeds. Valiantly throughout my life I would try to prove it wrong. Many times failure my determined companion.

The tongue I possessed was such a powerful weapon, it's appeal so sweet that it would enable me to uplift or destroy my friend and my enemy at my perceived leisure. True beneficiaries of my imagined refute yet rarely if ever could an apology be uttered.

Peculiar is life however for the heart as many knows will allow love, peace and understanding to enter it's domain. Here the mind reluctantly accepts change for tomorrow will come regardless of any shortcomings and always with a smile.

The sharing of my person, my treasures and my thoughts give me peace. For as I look at self, my shadow whispers you never failed because your heart softened and forgave you for causing it and others so much grief and pain. O' my last few breaths have never felt so good nor tasted so sweet. Thank you self and goodbye forever, for my eyes dear friend were finally opened though never are they to open . . . . ever again.

SPECIAL THINGS

From you a smile, it is why I live, a diamond with love, it is what I wish to give. Hope may be lost but I can dream, yes I can dream, it is the reason why I will always give you these special things.
Emeralds, rubies and pearls are gifts I will retrieve, for as long as I can love you, I will always believe.
We will take trips to all the exotic places and enjoy welcomes from the many royal faces.
All these things we will do for as long as I have you. Hope is sometimes woefully lost, but I can dream, it is the reason why I will always enjoy giving you special things.

WHEN ONE ASSUMES

When I look at them in anger, my hatred becomes a valued possession. Could I forgive him or even her if I am just as guilty of the same misdeed. Were it not committed against me I would eagerly say yes.

If I could kill him or her with my hatred or anger alone, would satisfaction cause my heart to smile with glee? Not a difficult choice dare I say for my thoughts and my want of retribution are so very poisonous, death to them is an agreeable conclusion.

If what I have concluded is wrong in its understanding, wrong in its interpretation, am I to allow them to explain their position concerning the matter of my perceived violation of trust? No for destruction is tasting so sweet in my mouth to the point of salivation.

If all of what I have assumed and have believed has guided me to error, while realizing my own transgressions are no different than theirs, do I allow her to come back to me and him to go about his way? After all he was a dear friend who merely wanted to repair our relationship. It is so amazing to me how jealousy can be so kind. I now find shame preparing my bed and jealousy smiling at its new fool.

SILHOUETTE

While cast against the glimmering moonlight, her lovely reflection graces the surface of the crystal clear lake. Her image as graceful as the flight of a swan.

Each movement of the water is a testament to her astounding beauty. Her silhouette is O' so stunning and breathtaking that it too appears to be alive.

Quietly two small fawns approach her, they too appear to be in awe of the reflection that rivals the beautiful moonlit night.

Secretly hidden from sight, I feel desires never felt among any that my life has ever experienced for such a creature has never been witnessed by me.

Eagerness assaults my every fiber, no longer able to hide, I give in to passion and approach her but from afar I hear the beating of wings. From the clouds a white stallion appears. Pegasus it seems is fast approaching.

As I get nearer to her, she mounts this magnificent animal and flies away. Left for me at the water's edge is is a white rose. I hear it saying someday she will return. I will patiently wait for you silhouette.

IMAGES

He is just an ordinary man, yet boastful pride is
his very essence. His treasures of ordinary value
are prized above any others that he may see.
A sense of respect being issued only to himself. In his
mind no one could ever be better.

His trappings of simple meaning impress only him,
since having friends means very little. There are
none whom he feels have enough material value
to be one of his companions.

Those who dare to converse with him are given a deaf
ear since rarely if ever does he heed any advice. In his
lust for superiority, how dare they assume to be his equal.

Self-indulgence is a coveted feeling, while being the focal
point of any attention or conversation always warms his
heart. In his mind the way he feels is a gift of life. Though for
those who are fortunate enough to know him, all see his life
is merely a charade.

A STROLL BY THE SEASHORE

Once on a windy and grayish day, I came upon an old man sitting alone by the seashore. Sir I asked, why do you sit here all alone?

Son he replied, I am waiting on time, I am going home. But you live there, yes you would not be remiss young man but where I will go is far, far nicer. You see young man I am you and you are me.

Saying good-bye I walked on though I decided to take a look back but noticed the old man was gone.

I soon began to understand that I too would sit there someday for my turn to go home, because we must all one day take a stroll by the seashore.

LITTLE WAYFARER

A young child is hopelessly blinded by a sea of snow, though being left alone and foraging for food is not unknown to him. Hunger is the reason why he ceases to shiver. His determined spirit not allowing him to think about the brutal cold. Hope comes in so many forms, despair though, is his constant and only companion. Where a light shines before him, instinct urges him to follow. Revealed by the light's promise of nourishment is a warm home with a joyous family inside. Entrance cannot be gained for he knows he is akin to a vagrant and a beggar. Survival for such a young soul is a journey in futility. There is however, someone who always intervenes to care for his angels. Someone who will provide him with nourishment where none is to be found. Yes a child he is, a little wayfarer he has become, but he also is . . . . the Wayfarer's child.

FATHER

If wisdom were gold, you would have been
bestowed many, many wishes, for you have
granted all of our silly little wishes. Nothing
we ever asked of you was ever a bother, we
love you so, beautiful father.

Sometimes our souls would become so tired
and start to stray, yet you were always somewhere
around to help us through the day. We
always heard you say, stay strong my children
good things will come, all you need do is look
back to where you have come from. Nothing
we ever asked of you was ever a bother, we
love you so, beautiful father.

As the days would go by and we would have
not a friend, you would always be there for us
as the day came to an end. If there is a father
more special, he we have yet to see, for you
are truly special and to us you will always be.
Because nothing we ever asked of you was
ever a bother, we love you so . . . . our beautiful
father.

MR MOSES

There was a man, an indigent I'd say. Yes a bum
I'd met one cool winter day. Sir is this the life you
wish to choose?
O' yes young man for it is not some ruse. My name
is Mr. Moses you see, don't feel sorry, you could be
me. Mr. Moses began to tell a story of a people who
had struggled, had been mistreated.
Yet had hearts so strong they would not be defeated.
Young man do not feel sad because we suffered for
you, so your life could be better, and we all made it
too.
I listened intently and I began to understand. This was
not some barren spirit who no longer wanted to live,
no here was a wise old man with much more to give.
No he was not some old dirty person no one could stand,
just a gentle old soul who was a wonderful man.
He also spoke of the beatings, dogs, and water hoses, but
life looked out for him, a wonderful friend he is, this man
called Mr. Moses.

A LITTLE BOY

A little boy looked up into the sky. He then asked, Lord why do people hate, why do people die? He got no answer, no not right away. The Lord wanted him to think for a moment before he had his say. A little boy said Lord which way do I turn, which way do I go? Only you have the answer, only you would know. The Lord finally answered, little boy things are as they should be, for all you need do is pray and love me, and with these things inside you, you will always know and will always see.

WHEN I GROW UP

When I grow up I want to be a doctor, no a lawyer, or dentist I guess.
When I grow up I want to live in a big house, have a big car and a big truck.
When I grow up I want my little sister to smile every day and not cry all the time because our parents don't love us. She will live with me for all the time.
When I grow up I will say, mom and dad we still love you but you can't hurt us anymore.
I must go now because I hear my dad coming to beat us, one day we will be here no longer, thank God for heaven because we never got to grow up.

THE PRIDE OF A MAN

I have accused my loved one of wrongs she never
committed. An injustice forced upon her because
of jealousy. Her tears mean little for my accusations
have become so common.
This I believe is my way of keeping her in hand since
I never worry about how she feels. In my mind she
would still be guilty no matter what she has to say,
no explanation could ever placate me.
Could my fortune be told, I would have been forewarned
about the inevitable, her spoken and reluctant departure,
my eyes saying I can do far better than you.
Though with tears in her eyes, she sadly looked back,
gave a brief smile and continued to walk away.
With not enough courage to say I was wrong, I watched
as my most beloved leave my life forever.
My face was firm and filled with intense anger as I watched
her leave. My pride even allowed me to spew forth words
I did not mean. To this day I am still alone, unwilling to say
I care and unwilling to give in. A love lost because of the
pride of a man.

GUIDING LIGHT

There is a beacon, a hope that calms my stormy life. Something that has always shone brightly to guide my way. Often as a child I gave way to frustration but always your soothing words would caress my wounded spirit. When I needed a friend or when I needed an angel, your vibrant smile would lift my soul to new horizons. Whenever I was too tired to believe, you always promised that you would give me your dream. When home was no longer a place for me, you always kept the door ajar. Whenever I would lie down to sleep you always made those angry shadows disappear. You are so wonderful and are truly treasured. You are my guiding light for you are like none that I know, thank you mother.

THE LAST SUPPER

Little children in a ravaged land appear so weary, desolate and despaired, what a warm friend would a slice of bread make.

In the minds of these forsaken little ones, thinking about the pain of hunger is but a passing, since a warm meal would resemble a mountain of gold to them.

Many souls never feel the wretched agony of days without sustenance for most are accustomed to bountiful tastings. Tastings that these little ones can only dream of, for it is unlikely they will ever see them.

In the minds of many who are more fortunate, it is well regarded that the last supper was between Jesus and his disciples, in the minds of these little ones, it has never occurred, for they have yet to see . . . . their first supper.

MY DEAR DAD

My dear dad I write to ask how are you?
Where have you been?
What did I say, what did I do? My dear
dad I ask why did you leave home?
Why never a message and why you never
phoned?
My dear dad I write to ask why mother never
speaks your name, what caused this to happen,
what was it that's changed?
These are questions I really need an answer to you
know. You see I always wanted you to be the best
friend I ever had, this is from my heart, my dear
dad.

THANK YOU MOTHER

Thank you mother for all the wonderful years, for with your strength I've overcome all my fears. Thank you mother for giving my solemn face a place to rest, for there is no better place of comfort than upon your breast.
Thank you mother for giving me the will to stay the course and stand strong, for with your belief in me, I have weathered many days that were both stormy and long.
Thank you mother for wiping my teary eyes, it is your reassuring words that have helped me keep my dreams alive. And each time I give thanks to God, I realize there could never be another, no not like you, so thank you . . . . mother.

I MUST SAY GOODBYE

When you are gone, I patiently waited for your return.
Weary I must rest for my wait is long, my mind says to
stay but my heart says I must say goodbye.
Hoping you will call is often a visit in fantasy for it is so
rare an occurrence. Where are you now is a question of
which I have no answer for whenever you are near I
wonder if I'm happy or terribly sad.
You embrace me with such a warm and loving touch,
a gesture that only causes doubt in my mind. I look
into your eyes to find an answer, a clue as to what
may be wrong, yet your smile says I need not worry.
I'm so lonely and confused, yes I know you are here
now. My mind says to stay for I love you. My heart
O' love, tells me I need to go. I won't look back and
I say to you—goodbye.

WHEN THE ENEMY IS A FRIEND

Cancerous thoughts go through his mind while at the same time he gives warm smiles and hellos. Your solid foundation of trust is in danger of being destroyed because preparing for an enemy that yearns for your loved one Is far from thought.
One cannot defend the home where there is no feeling of betrayal evident. Your years of love and dedication placed in jeopardy by an enemy who's motives are yet to be revealed.
He is an assailant with access and permission to enter one's dwelling with a freedom that any thief would envy for he is a friend.
The smiles and warm assurances of your loved one are comforting in this quest to betray you for her eyes are always embracing your soul.
Though she has fallen victim to his world of promises, promises his kind will rarely keep, suspicions are easily removed because of her gentle embrace and O' so warm reassurances. With your mind at ease, his cancerous thoughts have become your nightmare and she Is now conquered. She is now victim to his false dreams and promises. Even here, with realization fast becoming evident, she leaves you behind for she is blinded by his sincere promise of eternal love.
All your suspicions and accusations proven true, committed by a comrade, an ally, one you could not see for the enemy is a friend.

BROKEN FENCES

When one feels it is worth it, a person may travel very far to make right what was once done so wrong to another. But pain sometimes will cloud the minds of those who have been wronged. It can be difficult at times to mend broken fences.

The wronged may wish to forgive in their minds, but anger and hurt however, will not allow them to change their hearts. Sometimes it can be difficult to mend broken fences.

The offender can say I'm so sorry and I love you, the offended on the other hand, may be unrelenting, it can be difficult at times to mend broken fences.

Should a loved one be driven away and closes the hearts' door, and if forgiveness is all but forgotten, then it it is evident that sometimes one cannot mend broken fences.

There are so many things we all can do and cause to change when sharing the gift of the written word. Lives can and have been changed by what someone has said or written. As I look back on my first book, Moments In Time, I am amazed that what I have written has inspired and/or helped others to move forward. It is truly a blessing and a gift from God to have such a special talent. I will always believe that tomorrow is a new opportunity to be great and to do something great. As I think about all that has inspired me over the years to write poetry, I see it as a reflection of all that my life has become. When I think about all the difficult times we had when I was a child, I now realize someone somewhere had it far worse so I smile at those tough times and now consider them great memories. The foundation that I had supporting me then was truly remarkable. One person I will always love and remember was my grandfather. He did a great deal with very little and molded me into the man I have become. He was a great grandfather indeed. The other person that has given me all they had and more was my mother. Here was a woman that shared her gift of writing with me and sacrificed everything she had for me to get to where I am. Mom my work is dedicated to you because there is nothing I can do or say to express how much I love you and miss you. There ain't no words.

Made in the USA
Coppell, TX
28 November 2023